KNOWN BY SALT

ANHINGA PRESS

for Jim

The Philip Levine Prize for Poetry

The annual competition for the Philip Levine Prize for Poetry is sponsored and administered by the M.F.A. Program in Creative Writing at California State University, Fresno.

2017
Tina Mozelle Braziel
Known by Salt
Selected by C. G. Hanzlicek

2016
Rachel Rinehart
The Church in the Plains
Selected by Peter Everwine

2015
Andrea Jurjević
Small Crimes
Selected by C. G. Hanzlicek

2014
Christine Poreba
Rough Knowledge
Selected by Peter Everwine

2013
Chelsea Wagenaar
Mercy Spurs the Bone
Selected by Philip Levine

2012
Barbara Brinson Curiel
Mexican Jenny and Other Poems
Selected by Cornelius Eady

2011
Ariana Nadia Nash
Instructions for Preparing Your Skin
Selected by Denise Duhamel

2010
Lory Bedikian
The Book of Lamenting
Selected by Brian Turner

2009
Sarah Wetzel
Bathsheba Transatlantic
Selected by Garrett Hongo

2008
Shane Seely
The Snowbound House
Selected by Dorianne Laux

2007
Neil Aitken
The Lost Country of Sight
Selected by C.G. Hanzlicek

2006
Lynn Aarti Chandhok
The View from Zero Bridge
Selected by Corrinne Clegg Hales

2005
Roxane Beth Johnson
Jubilee
Selected by Philip Levine

2002
Steven Gehrke
The Pyramids of Malpighi
Selected by Philip Levine

2001
Fleda Brown
Breathing In, Breathing Out
Selected by Philip Levine

Contents

Acknowledgments

Thank you to the editors of publications where these poems first appeared, sometimes in earlier versions or attributed to Tina Mozelle Harris, my maiden name.

Appalachian Heritage: "Hydrangea Ridge" and "To Shake Another"

Auburn University Graphic Design Program Print for the Third Thursday Poetry Series at the Jule Collins Smith Museum of Fine Arts (Broadside): "Trailer Fish"

Aura: "Mozelle's Shoes"

Birmingham Arts Journal: "Known by Salt"

Birmingham Poetry Review: "Fluidity"

The Cincinnati Review: "Everywhere Welcome"

Construction: "Mama Said Nothing Good"

Coosa Riverkeeper Newsletter: "On Lay Lake"

Duende: "Homemaking," "To the Coosa River at Clear Springs Marina and Trailer Court," "Trespassing," "Clear View," and "Not Most"

Doggone: "Survival Biscuit"

Sister City Connection Anthology (Green Bucket Press): "Interview, 1966" and "The Finishing Work"

Grub Street Grackle: "Owing Nothing"

James Franco Review: "Allure" and "Song"

Jelly Bucket: "Beneath the Trailer"

The MacGuffin: "Homebuilding"

Pidgeonholes: "Fadeaway Girl" and "I've Learned"

PMS poemmemoirstory: "The Afterlife of Pine"

Raleigh Review: "To Season"

Southern Humanities Review: "Dog in the Road"

Tampa Review: "Looking Glass"

Rooted by Thirst (Porkbelly Press): "Birding," "Claims," "House Warming," and "Housekeeping"

"Known by Salt" was the state poetry winner for the 2016 Hackney Literary Awards.

Thank you, Jim, for your love and making our home-building and writing-life possible and such a delight. Mom, Dad, JJ, my uncles (Gene, Sam, Brent) and aunts (Trish, Marine, Mary, Am); thank you for your example and stories that inspire me and made me who I am. Mozelle, when the family says, "We didn't name you Mozelle for nothing," I take it as the highest praise. Delano, Dylan, and Madi, thank you for your help making Hydrangea Ridge home. Thank you, Ada, for making your home mine and mine yours.

Deep gratitude goes to my teachers at the University of Oregon; Danny Anderson, Garrett Hongo, and especially, Geri Doran; y'all are the best. Sincere thanks to William Logan for his continued guidance. Thank you, Tony Crunk, Bob Collins, and Bill Cobb, for all you taught me. Thank you very much, Kathrine Webb, Alicia Clavell McCall, Kerry Madden, Wendy Reed, Shelly Cato, Ashley Jones, and especially Lauren Slaughter, for your thoughtful feedback on these poems and, most of all, for your friendship.

I appreciate the Alabama State Council on the Arts for supporting this project with a fellowship. Thank you, Sewanee Writers' Conference, for the MFA scholarship. I deeply appreciate the encouragement from Claudia Emerson and Robert Hass. Thank you, Preston Browning, for the time and solitude to work on this collection at Wellspring House.

Thank you, Anhinga Press and Lynne Knight, for creating a lovely book to hold these poems. And thank you, Richard Bickel, for permitting me to use your wonderful photo for the cover. I am deeply and forever grateful to C. G. Hanzlicek, Connie Hales, and everyone at Fresno State for selecting *Known by Salt* for the 2017 Philip Levine Prize for Poetry.

KNOWN BY SALT

TRESPASSING

Relocate the bedrock in the threshold …
Make your study the unregarded floor.
— Seamus Heaney

Homemaking Along Lay Lake

So more will blossom beside the trailers next year,
the dahlia bulbs need to be dug and spread.

People here say they are *going to the house*
and drive back to their doublewides.

Home is made by repairing wooden piers for lot rent.
Made by cucumber and squash

that bridge well beyond their beds.
No one pays for muscadines, they're for jelly.

Watch that sunburnt kid. She dips paper boats in motor oil,
drops them in the lake to see them spin in ever-widening circles.

Dahlias swing, shovels dig their bulbs. Home is made
as the pressure cooker whistles through a singlewide.

Made under that throng of willow flies,
made where piers hammer us to this drift of blossoms.

Known by Salt

Instead of sugar, salt spangles my grapefruit halves,
cream of wheat, grits. Always salt on watermelon.

I get looks, questions for salting before tasting.
A habit of my father, his father and brothers.

Ironworkers, their jobs demanded salt,
offered in capsules that they never took.

The day I was born my father cut
from the carton the Morton salt girl

for me, his first-born, a girl,
whose salt pours under umbrellas.

I've never welded, never raised a bridge,
but I'm one of them in the taste we share

for what we get and need to take.

Beneath the Trailer

When I squatted beneath a trailer, a neighbor's or ours,
        wearing only Underoos
    and clutching a near-empty bag of Wonder Bread,

I wasn't just hiding from Mama,
        her hollering for me
    to put a dress on.

I sought a dark frontier,
        a cool shadow,
      long and wide as a home,
beyond Mama's heavy footfalls circuiting kitchen and den.

Where wheels bloomed with rust,
        I mapped trails
      over the gold glint of pine straw, through the grass,
to the river I needed to ford.

Underpinning thwarted that.
        Hung like a stiff bedskirt, it hid the sagging pipes,
      the hollows dogs dug to bear puppies,
those abandoned G. I. Joes.

It kept me out and was meant to
        keep me from dreaming my way West,
      from circling the trailers each night.

I didn't go anywhere.
        I squatted.
    I lay on down.

Trespassing

Why Grandma Mozelle took me trespassing
through half-built houses, I can't be sure.

As if "because we can" was reason enough,
she often said nobody thinks of women and children
as thieves or vandals.

I caught her sometimes sliding a hand over a countertop,
pretending, perhaps, to wipe away crumbs.

Maybe she just wanted to read me
the house frames: the studs of entry and barrier.

Among their barred shadows, she asked
if I could picture a window seat instead of that extra closet
or this dining room open to kitchen and den.

I kept busy shuffling sawdust, searching for the metal discs
that electricians punch from power boxes.

I didn't grasp the value then of recognizing walls,
looking through them, seeing other ways that they could lie.

To me, the prize was naming and numbering,
first, those coin-sized blanks,
then later, homes I wished to claim.

On Lay Lake

1. Swimmer

Like a daughter who has not forgotten
the world of her mother's body,

I know this lake, the springs
veining her with cold, each splash

an attempt to get outside herself.
I know her wavering reflections ask:

is this how sky looks in that tree,
is this how still your home sits.

2. Dissenter

This lake ain't nothing
but a river fattened

within a stall. The river
is its hidden muscle, its bone.

The dam holds
what bit it can

while the river paws
at its foundation.

No one fights
a river and wins.

3. The River

Call me Coosa,
for I won't answer

to the stagnant thud of Lay Lake,
Logan Martin, or Neely Henry.

Call me Coosa, confluence
of Etowah and Oostanaula.

Bring back what is sinuous:
those syllables, my meander

through Alabama,
when Alabama meant thicket.

4. Former Farmer, Now Trailer Park Owner

I know the lake as bottom
where I once grew collards,

dark waves of them rippling
where that ski boat plows past those piers.

Now I harvest lot rent
from folks wanting nothing more

than to plant themselves
between my pines.

5. Fisherman

Along the riprap, casting a rod
for bass or crappie, I watch

the drift of the lake, its scaled skin,
water seeping into stone, rising into air,

moving through flesh. A serpent.
The lake a mere bend of its body.

Mama Said Nothing Good

would come from bad beans: the shriveled
and darkened ones that she culled

from what would be our dinner. Still, I planted them
in a caldron of dirt, not caring if the soil raised them upright.

Mama said I'd amount to nothing
if I didn't start caring how things look.

She said that we can't rinse the dirt from our blood —
not looking bad is all we got.

When those beans sprouted white-green curls
— the hair of mermaids drowning in the dirt —

I took it as proof that what is bad is just something good
appearing where it shouldn't. I figured it

would take the power of Moses for those struggling creatures
to part the red clay, swim on down to a good sea.

Mama predicted that they'd choke,
that this is how something bad takes care of nothing good.

Trailer Fish

Unlike the stray cat apartment
and the clapboard horse, the trailer

is cold-blooded: windows open like gills,
sides swim and heave in the wind.

No one chooses a trailer park aquarium
over a cul-de-sac corral.

When the dam breaks and flooded houses
stand as steadfast as the neighboring pines,

the trailer hitch juts out as proudly
as the lip of Elizabeth Bishop's fish.

Toss it back, watch its unblinking eye sink,
see the Airstreams rise like bluegill,

listen to the shady hum
of doublewides gliding by.

Pins

A tack, bobby pin, or finishing nail
        mouth-held
    by anyone

makes Mozelle shudder and beg,
    "Don't
    scare me like that."

Her mother, as a young girl,
        appears
    like a worn memory,

laying her doll out on a rough table
        while pinching
    a dress pin between her lips.

Motes swirl around her,
        slivering
    the afternoon hush.

Startled by a knock, her chin
        jerks,
    and the dress pin plunges.

She bends, coughs, but can't
        get it
    to come back up.

Decades later, a doctor slips it from her throat, lifting
        the pin
    like a splinter. What does he grasp,

spite or insignificance? Does he suspect its lack
            or abscess,
      how forty years gone,

Mozelle still wants the pin
          that killed
      her mother? Not to hold on to malice.

She wants it like my father wanted
          the ladder rung
      that gave, the one he clung to

as he fell fifty feet, the rung
          whose hollow throat
      he clutched in the ER,

hardhat upturned in his lap to catch
          blood streaming
      from shattered jaw and arm.

His desire was to take
          measure,
      fling it away.

Keepsakes are other things —
          the pin
      placed in his elbow, the one he asked for

when his surgeon dug it out,
          is now kept
      in a bowl where he drops his change

and soapstone at night. Thinner than a pencil,
        it holds
     the weight of rebar,

that bit of steel
        that held
     and gave mend.

To Season

Now let me praise parsley, the pause of leaf,
on the 99 cent Stuckey's breakfast plate,

my first encounter with the emerald furl
beside grits and fried egg. Praise it

as a harbinger of this flat-leaf parsley palming
my white wine and buttered penne.

Let me praise rosemary, watch it curve into laurels
above ears of corn now roiling in the pot.

Praise the fragrant fronds I had known only as a weed
in Mozelle's story of how she tucked rosemary

into the neck of her meal-sack dresses.
Let me praise its perfume allure for sating her

longing for glamour when she lacked lacquers
to redden her nails and gloss her lips.

Now praise us, salt (you mineral),
sing of grit, hum as you rise from our pores.

Praise us as we sharpen our knives, cure
these iron skillets. Let praise distinguish us,

place us here but coming from there;
let praise *now* us, bring us into this season.

ALLURE

For there is no creature whose inward being is so strong
that it is not greatly determined by what lies outside it.
— George Eliot

Allure

1. Suede

Nude before the mirror, she scrutinizes
her sapling legs and the ant-bite swell of breasts.

She fingers the gold sequined thong,
then steps into it the way she'd cross a low wall.

Sliding into heels, she grasps her hips.
Sashay, she thinks, sashay

like the harried Bugs Bunny sways
until Elmer Fudd goes walleyed.

The suede bra tsk-tsks shut
between her breasts.

She struts around an imagined pole
and down the hall to her roommates.

Karma clinches it, says, "You'll kill
them at the club."

While Ty says nothing,
his irises widening into a dark sea.

She must be a lithe rabbit now,
swift to elude, twitching her hips

until each Elmer Fudd changes
from a hunter with a gun

to a hunter without one.

2. Blush

Watch Elmer Fudd's face bloom pink,
     his cheek dropping to his shoulder,
          when Bugs Bunny bats his eyes,

lifts one knee above the other,
     softening into that feminine bend
          to the looking glass.

Hear the mirror crooning, "Hey, girl, turn
     your head, arch your back.
          It's that easy to make him sigh for you."

See Bugs blot his lips. See him boost his bustle.
     Hear Elmer murmur, "Isn't she lovely."
          Watch him clasp his hands beneath his chin.

3. Formica

Her table is set: vegetable soup brims red bowls,
glasses of tea sweat on the blue Formica,
the cornbread exhales its golden brown.

Outside the baby's room, she cracks the door
to look in. She hears her husband talking
on the porch. What his friend says about her

she doesn't quite catch: her good cooking or looks.
Her husband hears something double-edged in it
(just Sunday pretty, not a Friday night fox), a barb

needling him to boast, "That and she was a stripper."
"Shit, I knew from looking," his friend replies.
Heat crackles her face. His eyes will fall on her

as blunt as a chisel. Even now she feels
her husband's gaze sweeping over her,
a sculptor's hand sanding the arc of her hip.

She waits for a coolness to rise within,
like that of marble, how Galatea must have felt
while she was still stone.

4. Salome

I unzip my skirt and unsnap my suede bra.
The stage lights veil the stares and smiles.

In silhouette, men lift pints of beer.
Those shadows never reach me.

I see a guy's eyes only if he stands by the stage,
holds dollars at his chest, shy boy offering a bouquet.

When he bites a bill, I bend to pluck it with my teeth.
Our lips touch nothing but the dollar's calla lily furl.

I don't feel him when I run my fingernails
along his jaw or toss my hair over his shoulders.

When he lifts a rolled dollar towards my hip,
I snap my g-string over a paper finger

that never pulls the thin fabric down,
never traces the curve of my waist.

Then he is gone, folded back
into the row of paper dolls lining the walls.

Under the lights, my shadow multiplies,
each another petal blossoming from my feet.

Later, I smooth dollar after dollar flat.
Each pictures the head of a bodiless man,

from each rises a perfume not quite floral
more of a musk muddled by thousands of hands.

Interview, 1966

Even in Burger King's dim office, grease festered.
Mozelle did not wave it away. Striding past the fryers'

crackling static, through the swinging doors,
she sat before the owner could stand.

She did not take a cigarette from her purse
or the pack he offered. When he asked, "Divorced?"

she nodded. Said she'd done inventory and set schedules
for the cooks and busboys at a steakhouse

her ex-husband was now running alone.
She smoothed her houndstooth suit,

taking in how each check stepped from one square into another.
When he pushed up his glasses and asked,

"So what, then, did your husband do there?"
her smile straightened into a silent line.

"Sorry. I'm not hiring a woman. I'm not
coming down here to change every light bulb."

Mozelle stood, then stepped onto his desk.
Taking hold of the ceiling fixture,

she unscrewed the bulb. He just stared, lips agape,
ready to swallow that glass pear whole.

He wouldn't dare look up her skirt.
Does it matter that she got the job?

Fadeaway Girl

It's not a question of what kind of person flies and what kind of
person fades … the question is … Who do you want to be, the
person you hope to be, or the person you fear you actually are?
— John Hodgman

More than bluegill and their rising scent,
more than oak leaves drifting or mirrored,

a lake holds sky: blue blending to blue,
clouds billowing among the ripples.

So swimming is how a girl
has it both ways: secret and soaring,

swayed by a sinuous sky
that veils as much as it wombs.

Song

What gleams? A pearl:
orbit of opulence
hardened around a sliver
of salt or a slight crag of sand,

the singing moon
wooing lover to lover:
Come a little bit closer,
let me bite your lip.

Come morning the cotton
goes to the gin (a burr hidden
in the cloudy whisper of bolls)
and purple hulls fill my bowl.

The hulls open to strands
of peas, each a pale bead
with a dark eye peering
from green sheen.

Besides shine
what is pearl
but some grit

an oyster turned round
and round, wishing
she could spit?

The Nothing that Is

M aybe it's the wind, its hiss
like a spigot's.
Or the buzzard's glide
through the valley, wings rippling
like a stingray. Or maybe the waver
of bare branches brings
some belief in buoyancy
and this longing to rise.
Maybe it's the hiss,
"You can, can't you,
taste it, that soaring?"
that is the wind's goading
or maybe it is me saying it
and sighing, "If only,
I took it between my teeth."

I've Learned

with frogs, a kiss risks a prince.
Galant, for sure. But so ga-ga
for ribboned ringlets and lace
flounces that a girl changes,
arranging herself like a tray.

A lizard, though, doesn't ask
for nothing. Another species?
Three thousand times his size?
Wear a dress so tight I look
like a can of busted biscuits?
He pushes up, flares his throat.

And for that
knee-taut, hip-sure, belly-slack,
nude-without-nakedness ease,
I say, hey babe, fuck me.
Make me that undone.

Movable Objects

Tonight, luminescent algae lights the shore.
The water gleams like a starry sky.
Its glints swirl away before I can touch them.

Nights long ago I stretched out on the sand
and watched meteors cross the sky, wanting to rearrange

the low-slung stars, those immovable objects,
into a gondola gliding beneath an arched bridge
and a peacock spreading his iridescent fan.

I'd wanted to rid the sky (map of my days)
of arrows, bullish horns, scorpion stings.

This morning, the water rocked me
as if I were its only baby. But the sky surfed
with clouds did not mirror me in its blue.

Who wants that sky or these lights stirring
in dark waters as if every movement is an irresistible force?

Give me this sand that wind sways into dunes,
give me the shore lifting
around the shape of my footsteps.

Let the surf smooth it into a flat mirror
reflecting the blue light of the moon.

Tornado Sermon

For three days now we have cleared rubble,
boarded windows, carried each other so no one sits
        like Job in the ashes of what was.

        We have found mounds of shoes,
heaped round the pipes and brick of what once was a home:
        each shoe without its mate,
all the others flung across the county
        except one pair, a pair with the laces tied together.

We have stared at a mirror
        reflecting a darkening sky,
a mirror hung on the only wall left
        testifying that a house once stood there.

And we have asked ourselves:
        why do we find stobs of load bearing walls,
the tangle of sheets and insulation, when an untouched home
        stands across the street?

        How can china cups remain on their hooks
above an overturned stove?

        How else can we answer, but to say,
this isn't the work of a dumb creature.
        We know the wind is a woman,
staunch and unwavering.

        We know her seething songs,
deepening into hum and rumble as roofs rise,
        as plywood knocks against car hoods
in a deadly cadence,

a music that demands we lay hands on
what we treasure,
        and let all else swirl away.

We must turn, sway,
        wrap arms around another's waist,
lace ourselves together like that pair of shoes,
        and we must waltz.

Hold tight, so many are still breaking.

        Like my sister, who fled
her trailer and sheltered in a neighbor's cabin.
        She watched the logs pull away,
felt herself lifted, then dropped in a nearby field.
        Her arm broken.
Her son's back pierced.

        Hold onto her,
hold back the breaking
        from carrying her son
and her neighbor's body, from carrying on
        as strangers drove by taking pictures.

Go to the house on Baker's street,
        where the kitchen is torn away,
find hanging on tiny hooks teacups, that fine china,
        as delicate as a chicken bone,
find a cup waiting there for you, for me,
        for all of us,
a cup that won't pass us by.

We've searched fallen oak and briers
       for chickens, littered fields for photographs.
We've seen ourselves in that mirror.
       Now we've got to search ourselves
like we searched broken planks
       and fallen chimneys for moan and movement
for someone we might save.

Holiday Lights at Palisades Park

"Johnny Waites is gone ..." a poster says
beside a scarecrow holding a cane pole,
"gone fishing, 1954-2013."

Nearby white lights spell out *Live with Passion*
as if this were the reason for the season
instead of the illumination of tree branches.

Of course, there's baby Jesus lying
in the gazebo. Here's Santa. And up ahead,
Snoopy rounds out the Christmas trinity.

Although signs advertise Hyde Medical Supply
and Pine Bluff Baptist, it isn't clear
who wound which lights into reindeer.

But the abominable snowman must be
"in memory of Granny Goodlow"
because a girl lays flowers at his feet.

Look, where the picket fence opens to a white carpet
lit with electric stars. See that figure clad
in camouflage cradling a compound bow?

Wings lift from his back, but his stance says
his passion for the dark woods will carry him beyond
these lights and sheets of tulle hung around him.

Evolution of Stone Veneer

Without drapes, the windows stare
dumbly at the sapling shadows
branching across the yard

mapping how it could have gone
and not come to this.
A notice tacked on the door

black and white as a banker's suit.
Mattresses thrown in a mound
with a brand new Scrabble board

and Crock-Pot at the drive's end.
Until now, who knew it wasn't real,
the walls' veneer, the tenants slipping

so far under water? If only they had hauled
their own river rock. True stone holds on.
Or at least, it knows to look away.

Survival Biscuit

It's small thanks, naming snapper throats, okra, and collards,
when the man ringing me up asks, "What'd you eat?"

Beside his register, a tin of Survival Biscuit, USDA Ration.
"I found that in an old fallout shelter," he tells me,

proud that Niki's Meat and Three can keep serving
even in the black rains of nuclear winter.

As a child I never saw rations, only the yellow fallout sign
and neighbors hunched in courthouse pews. Savoring

the butterscotch Life Savers that someone passed around,
we kids pooled pocket change for a Yoo-hoo.

Upstairs, the clatter of typing meant tornadoes had not siphoned
our world away. I shelter in the butteriness of then and now

as I step to the door and someone — the waitress I know
only as Jill or the woman behind the steam table

whose eyes I barely met hungering for black-eyed peas
and okra — calls out, "Come on back, hon."

To the Coosa River at Clear Springs Marina and Trailer Court

Come evening, all tilts towards you,
light sifts down until your waters hold
more sheen than the sky.

Herons lift their backward knees
along your banks as egrets flock
to festoon the pines.

Like an outboard whining its way
across your slough, then settling
into an idle hum beside its pier, I linger,

wanting to hear your whisper hushing
the trailers and me. I long to stay
and feel the boat's wake kiss the fall-away shore.

Today I swam to the island, scratched
between the horns of the goat who *baas*
his lonesomeness and again

I was young and at home. I walked
beneath pines once whitened
by so many birds, their weight bent

the boughs beyond buoyancy.
Tomorrow I drive cross country,
making my way to settle beside another river.

I hear its waters run north and cold, too cold
for swimming. Don't hold on to me
like a mother, don't lay out this silken shine.

Let me go, but come with me,
set my body atilt with your sway
each night. Can't you shift like the egrets

who rearrange themselves from one branch
to another, each nearness shining
as perfect as the last and the next?

When It Strikes

Back home when a rush of wind blew the mist away,
though some wisps (soft nothings that bolls whisper

to one another) stayed woven into the rows of cotton.
And when pines swayed, leaning in to eavesdrop,

we knew the sky meant what it said —
the bleach-blue light eddying around us could strike.

Dad told me how a thunderbolt found
and left him crumpled inside

a phone booth. Mom says, *Oh darling that was nothing
but a jolt of love. Weren't you calling me to say good night?*

Dad says he saw it, saw it coming,
like a mercurial wave rippling down the phone line.

But I didn't see mine coming, not out here,
not so far from you, where the sky hides

behind a mist that doesn't blow away
but hangs on spider threads.

There's no sun glistering this haze.
Like this sky, I tried to hide my fracturing,

but when I saw you, your gaze traveling
over the horizon through the screen of my phone,

I couldn't hide how that flash of you
runs through me. Like tributaries flooding the sky.

Everywhere Welcome

Because the drummer's tap
of the high-hat sets air atremble.

Because the fragrance of rosemary
lingers on hands that fondle its fronds.

Because within the thrill of chocolate
lies a taste something like bread — its dark

subsistence. Because pink light and pale blue
shadow render Mount Rainer as tender

as a breast, aloft and untouched above the haze.
Because beauty startles — the tang of fried pickles,

that dirt-sex scent of tomatoes. Because every crevice
in snow glows blue even in shadow, that aqua blue

of water swirling up to fill limestone quarries.
Because Mozelle's warble resonates

with the echoing clack of pool balls as they roll
through the table's trough and her cadence

brings to mind the bliss of spring breezes
that neither warm nor cool — just slide silken

over skin whenever she sings that ditty
about how blue jays whistled

and buzzards danced when that old cow
died in the middle of the branch.

WHAT IT TAKES

… drawing out soreness
from the swells, removing splinters, taking
whatever hands will give.
— Natasha Tretheway

A Clear View

Neighbors talked, saying, "That Mozelle,
she is going to get her a house."

Not quite "bless her heart,"
yet scant admiration for a woman

mixing mortar with her groom
the day after their wedding.

Brick withstands such huff and puff
at a divorcee marrying a brick mason

her daddy's age, at a couple moving
into a half-built house three blocks from Main.

That was the 1950s. And now
I'm another Mozelle building a home

after wrecking his so we can live
like bears in the woods.

I hold panes in place,
while my husband secures their frames.

We're raising a glass cabin
for its clear view on whatever

a neighbor may think
or decide to hurl our way.

Hydrangea Ridge

1.

With chainsaw and sling blade, we felled pine and hickory,
slung away brier and poke. Together we string our squarings.
Dig in with auger, rock bar, and shovel.

Dig to embed our pole foundation. Each morning
the suckerings bend the squaring lines and another toad squats
in a hole, presiding over its shallow puddle.

We have to lie down to scoop him out. He stays close,
ready to reclaim his deep and narrow kingdom.

2.

The mantis prays on the pane.
Above the stove, webs fill with mosquitoes and moths.
A walking stick strolls over porch screens.

Outside, in the thicket of fleabane daisy and brier,
a tomato volunteered its vine, bore fruit.
Spiny branches shelter it from hungry deer.

When the king snake slipped away from the house,
we called for it to come back,

come back for the kitchen mice, for chipmunks,
for the rattlers that we fear nestling in the woodpile.

3.

A chill rises, the leaves blaze
as if to warm the trees' shivering limbs.
We turn, orbiting closer to the woodstove.

From felled trees we haul rounds to their cradle.
Then we circle the radiating dark iron,
reaching out to take hold of its heat.

Outside, no breeze stirs, still the bare trees sway,
flickering from all that burns within,
the days of grasping after sun, gleaning its fire.

To Shake Another

When heat visibly wavers over our truck hood,
we feel like puddles, our skin as thin as a frog's.

From the broom sedge, the rattle of katydids ripples
through us. I first felt sound in grade school

when a struck tuning fork touched another.
Its quaver shook the other fork into its own humming.

Evenings then, when pines shivered
with the chirr of peepers,

I wondered how frogs carry
quivering metal inside their tenderness.

Today pressing my cheek to our house frame,
I hammer, listening to how all the driven nails resound.

Each strike deepens the note ringing out
from here to beyond the ridge.

In it, I feel the reverberation
of hammer, anvil, and stirrup

of when he first called my name setting
what is tender and mettle in me abuzz.

House Warming

At dinner parties, my husband knocks on sheetrock
and plaster alike, testing the tensile strength of walls
and the space between studs. When his fingers wrap

around my wrist the way he grasps his hammer,
he will ask what I want: exposed rafters, a skylight,
maybe a transom tilting above our front door.

Once he asked the hostess if her office had been painted
for a nursery. He didn't mean it as a face-slap.
He meant nothing more than a guy swapping a shoulder slug,

measuring how far he can take what someone gives.
On the drive home, he wished their basement
sunk deeper and the attic beams hoisted higher

as if then, those living there could pack away regret.
If only they widened their sleeping porches
they might rest easy, chins tucked over fists.

No Cause for Prediction

For meteorologist James Spann

It's been sixty-three dry days.
Wind rummages the trees. Leaves no longer rustle
but surge and gush, a rattling sort of solace.
Peepers have gone hoarse goading the sky for water.
Dust stirs, smoke rises, taking humidity's place
in hazing the horizon.

The forecaster says we need moisture to draw rainfall,
meaning our lack is a downward spiral.
He could say drain, evoke its swirling sink.
Instead, he says drought, then severe drought
turning exceptional. "Noccalula and Desoto Falls
are bluffs now." Black Creek and the Little River
reduced to a series of ponds.

Bluffs he can say for certain, pictures prove it,
unlike all that climate hype predicting what isn't settled.
He won't say downpour or thunderstorm.
He won't moisten my parched mouth
by sucking a dry stone.

The Afterlife of Pine

Once hewn and planked, oak savors its past:
relics of sap river down a board's length;
at each end, rings circle rings sanctifying an acorn's drop.

In Raleigh long ago,
horsetail brushes combed a faux oak finish
over pine banisters and walnut walls —

workmen even costumed
the rectory's oak doors
with their own oaken flourish.

Now our house frame resurrects pine:
the studs branch at right angles
and nails dam boards into running flush.

Such cloistering fails to preserve wood's fluidity:
how trunks sway, twigs fork, leaves spill,
how trees well up to flood the sky.

What It Takes

M oving in meant knowing the house from its bones.
Not settling in or settling for the lay of the rug
on subfloor or the mirror hung from exposed beams.

It meant taking up moving. The bed
from this corner to that, so the scaffolding could roll past.
So we could wake to an angle the light slants in.

We became nomads, forever moving
to take what the climate and terrain
of the house would give.

This meant another sort of care,
more than measuring twice and cutting once
or letting tools rest wherever they lie.

It means giving
whatever muscle
comfort takes.

Breaking and Entering

Since hummingbirds light on our crossbeams
and lizards traverse the floor,
our home seems more pavilion than house.

No breaking needed, we joke.
No reason to barricade the doorway,
when cat or burglar can enter through gaps between studs.

Then we woke to hoofstep inside our house.
We dared not breathe, the doe might spook
and bolt through a newly hung pane.

We laid still, imagining the elegant lift of her neck,
her ears turning before she turned.
We were struck by her ease crossing our threshold

as if it were nothing, our roof, a crude and low sky.
Struck, too, by how quickly we'd forgotten fear,
how it can jolt us into breaking from what we've entered.

Not Most

"Most women wouldn't live without running water."
A compliment, maybe backhanded, or a challenge.

Most likely a warning against giving up the ease
of a warm shower or a mirror's sink. But I'm not Eve

walking away from garden and God just to feel the sway
between the good of having and the evil of not.

It's beguiling though, the black racer I found
while trudging through our woods.

Startled, she slinked so lithe over fallen branch and leaf,
her swift glide seemed more blessing than curse.

I've given arms and legs for such deft swerves.

The Finishing Work

takes the longest, some visitors warn, taking in my lack
of cupboards, flooring, and interior walls.

Longest, meaning forever.

I think of the finishing done by old-time schools
and by my grandmother staining kitchen cabinetry.

Finishing, meaning unquenchable thirst
of girls and wood grain for more,

more lacquer or stain, a gloss worn like mail,
armor against threats of being forever undone.

I Took His Name

B ecause I could.
Because he told me to
"pronounce it like the country."
And I wanted that.

I'm rewriting tradition,
calling myself Conquistador,
venturing from my mother's house,
to take the place I want.

Yes, there were x's
as in the spot,
as in lovers, boyfriends,

all those marks made
while my heart was still
becoming literate.

Work Shirt

It is sky: fading denim,
a ravel of clouds along cuff and collar,
each pearl snap another rising moon.

And that sky is my father: he laid steel in it,
claiming high territories for bridges
and penthouse suites, traversing thin I-beams

with nothing steadying him but the pale blue.
My father handed that down to me.
Yes, it's huge and soft worn like suede.

Something worn to bed and out at bars.
But now that I'm framing the windows of my home,
it suits me as if it were my own blue skin.

Homebuilding

I pull the screen taut. Your arm lifts
and falls, tacking screen to the frame
whose wood will slowly swell and silver.

With wide-spread hands, you press
the frames into place, ardent to drop the latch
into its eyelet and feel screened in.

Leaning my forehead on the tiny squares,
each another border claiming the red of an oak leaf,
a dogwood's gnarled turn, the hydrangea bloom as ours,

I see us in each one: clearing brush,
spreading a quilt on a sunlit slope, tying
the clothesline between hickory and house.

RIVERING

Anything is enough if you know how poor you are.
You could step out now in wonder.
                                    — Larry Levis

Trash

My neighbor burns his beside his trailer.
A garbage truck picks up ours,
but we have no plumbing.
I can't say who is poorer.

But his stinks,
a singed outlet smell that makes me worry
that some base electrical fire hides in our walls.

It brings back my grandparents' pile burning
beside the scrawny tomatoes Mom forbid me to eat,
the sprawling squash Dad backed over
because it grew so close to the rutted drive,

and the roses Ma-Maw bedded and moated
with long stretches of lawn.
One vine grew over the bay window
of her doublewide as if netting a big catch of pretty.

"Lipstick on a pig," is what my friend said once
pointing out red geraniums hanging from a trailer's porch.
A hedge fund banker, she had no idea where I come from.

That stunk too.

I don't know if it was her or me.
The trailer park chip on my shoulder,
the one my teacher said I should knock off,
smolders.

I do know what people say,
that others treasure what you throw out.

But I'm afraid I'm like my neighbor
unwilling to give another man mine.

Some treasures are just for me
to burn.

Claims

Everywhere we walk, orange signs warn
Private Property or *Posted.*

Still dented cans rattle in ditches and campfire rings,
claiming, "No, mine too."

And something in the surveyor's talk about tramping
over ridges and steeping himself in briers to sight the division

between neighbors, that thinnest of lines, a spidery net he casts
across the county — that, he claims, is his.

All the while, at the far reaches of our property,
the burr oak swells its bark over pig wire

and a sign more rusted than orange
reads: NO   SING.

And that fawn curled in the wood,
throat laid down beside side-turned hooves,

never flinched when our dog sniffed her.
She held her ground, or it held her.

Her dappled fur marked as belonging
to sunlight and fallen leaf.

Birding

Where lichen blooms green on the hickory.
Where an unblinking rabbit hunches

in his burrow. Where dried hydrangeas
and broom sedge rustle in the breeze.

I watched you carry an armload of oak
through the uphill brush and stack rounds

in the wood cradle. When the red hawk unfurled his cry
between bare branches, your eyes lifted and your lips parted.

I saw you breathe in his longing.
Watched it unfold, flowering in your chest.

Owing Nothing

After an evening of chop and haul,
kindling and banking fire,
it's easy to feel self-reliant.

Foxfire gives little light, no heat
as if it owes nobody nothing.
Burning in a parallel world,
only its glow filters into ours.

And the oak,
whose split limbs the foxfire brightens?
It mined sky for sun
ten hours a day for thirty-odd years.

And for what,
the moon-glow of a cold fire,
these logs that will burn into next week?
No. Nothing gives such industry away.

So there's that debt. Always that.

All Our Things Are Resurrections

R etired telephone poles sustain our deck,
and old church glass fills our windows.

From H's farmhouse, we salvaged
a tongue and groove heart pine ceiling for our floor.

This is more everyday than miracle
where dead hydrangea stems unfurl new leaves

and every sapling we plant (fig, crab apple, redbud)
dries up, dies, then comes back a spring or two later.

All our things are everyday
calling for me to wake

like water roused to wine,
like sand rousted into glass.

Rivering

When you say you will build me a river,
you sink a shovel and level planks.

I know you, your apron of nails,
the drill bits you leave scattered

around the house and yard.
Their ends are shaped like tiny daisies.

A river, you say, will make me happy
forever. And I think of our first day.

You spread my quilt in the sun.
I told you then it is all water:

the hill is wave; the field, a low pond.
You said I see that now.

And now I know rivers.
How they gully, smooth rock

to stone, slick mud.
How they bed by lying down.

Housekeeping

Each morning, a hummingbird
whirrs to the window to watch
the glass bloom with his likeness.

And I recognize the house is not kept
by sweeping straw across floor-planks
and rubbing rags over shelves.

I'd do better to lie in the hammock all day,
lifting a finger to the breeze
sieved through screen,

listening to the cat purr as he strolls
from corner to corner, smudging
the house with his thrum.

Mozelle's Shoes

When I say my feet won't fill her shoes,
I mean her snakeskin pumps,
her patent leather loafers, her suede boots.

I'm not using a metaphor to show you
how I'm unable to follow her footsteps.

I'd never pretend I could stand to go
deaf from scarlet fever, to go blind
from a husband's slap;

I couldn't make my way out
of the quiet, the dark to recover
sound and sight like she did.

I can wear her silk blouses, her belts
and rings, yet my feet aren't big enough

to sport one pair of the splendid shoes
that line her closet.

But when you call me by her name,
a name that sounds like the bounding
of a gazelle, my feet feel moccasined

in their own skin, and I know I can
leap any fence, run any distance.

Fluidity

For so long the world as water:
clouds billowing above the ridge
swell into the foam of ocean wave.

The window is a slow puddle.
Decades from now it ripples
from where I lean my head today.

A scientist on the radio
says the fluidity equation is as lovely
and constant for the rain eddying

in a ditch as it is for the swirl of galaxies.
But now I am turning from fluidity,
I see those clouds as dunes

built by windblown grit.
The ridge as a sandbank:
the bare trees are sea oats holding it in place.

Instead of the drifting rise and fall,
I want to remain here
running my fingers over the undulations

of your hair. Now the world as sea oat,
shooting through glass shards
and shifting sand, rooted by thirst.

Simple Machine

Like a stick levering a stone free
or a rope pulleying planters to our eaves
or a board ramping the impossible heft
of an iron stove up and into our truck bed,
our love is a simple machine.

Always at hand, taking out backbreak
by giving magnitude to our sway.
Love levering stove and pulleying bed,
love ramping us up beyond all eaves.

Looking Glass

Evening. Lamps stage-light the cabin.
Inside, the glass walls mirror their glare:

our loft bed hung in the clouds,
a tabletop rising from briers. I look

murky like the undulating girl
I saw while peering into the lake.

I try to see myself as dryad:
arms foliage patterned, neck

textured by bark. But I don't seep
into landscape or it doesn't rise in me.

Outside a luna moth frets the pane
while an armadillo rummages underbrush.

To see out, I look through my shadow.

Dog in the Road

After Brigit Pegeen Kelly

These are the shrinking days. Days of letting go.
May they go quick like the runoff that cuts ruts
in the road. May the basil go on now to seed.
And the tomatoes over-ripen and droop
on drying vines. And when the leaves turn brilliant
orange and scarlet, may their turning
from their branches be the mind shifting,
covering new ground. Like those evenings
when the eastern sky pinks and we watch
our neighbors' sunset. Like this evening:
the red clay glows peach and the gravel
gleams so blue that the road becomes sky
and the crow flying ahead is its own dog.

About the Author

Tina Mozelle Braziel, winner of the 2017 Philip Levine Prize for Poetry, directs the Ada Long Creative Writing Workshop at the University of Alabama at Birmingham. *Known by Salt* (Anhinga Press) is her first book. Her poems also have appeared in her chapbook, *Rooted by Thirst* (Porkbelly Press), and in *The Cincinnati Review, Southern Humanities Review, Tampa Review,* and other journals. She and her husband, novelist James Braziel, live and write in a glass cabin that they are building by hand on Hydrangea Ridge.